Anonymus

Joan of Arc

The Story of a Noble Life

Anonymus

Joan of Arc
The Story of a Noble Life

ISBN/EAN: 9783742826015

Manufactured in Europe, USA, Canada, Australia, Japa

Cover: Foto ©Andreas Hilbeck / pixelio.de

Manufactured and distributed by brebook publishing software (www.brebook.com)

Anonymus

Joan of Arc

JOAN OF ARC;

OR,

THE STORY OF A NOBLE LIFE.

Written for Girls.

> "Lo! where the holy banner waved aloft,
> The lambent lightnings play. Irradiate round,
> As with a blaze of glory, o'er the field
> It stream'd miraculous splendour."—SOUTHEY

> "Joan of Arc,
> A light of ancient France."—TENNYSON.

EDINBURGH:

WILLIAM P. NIMMO.

1871.

JOAN OF ARC;

OR,

THE STORY OF A NOBLE LIFE.

CHAPTER I.—HER EARLY YEARS.

"The hand of God is strong upon my soul,
And I have wrestled vainly with the Lord,
And stubbornly, I fear me. I can save
This country, Sir! I can deliver France!
Yea ... I must save the country!... God is in me;
I speak not, think not, feel not of myself.
He knew and sanctified me ere my birth;
He to the nations hath ordained me;
And whither *He* shall send me, I must go;
And whatso *He* commands, that I must speak;
And whatso is *His* will, that I must do;
And I must put away all fear of man,
Lest *He* in wrath confound me."

SOUTHEY, *Joan of Arc*, B. i.

IN order to understand the nature of the work to which JOAN OF ARC devoted herself in life and death, I must tell you something about the condition of France when she was born.

This was early in the fifteenth century, and France was then in a most pitiful condition. She was torn to pieces by the struggles of her own sons, and whilst these were fighting with one another, she was wholly unable to stop the conquering march of our English Henry the Fifth, who entered Paris, married the French king's daughter, and was afterwards crowned King of France. The capital was occupied by English troops. The fairest provinces were plundered by troops of armed brigands, who burned houses and pillaged granaries. There appeared on every hand nothing but confusion, poverty, desolation, solitariness, and fear. "The lean and bare lábourers in the country," says an old writer, "terrified even thieves themselves, who had nothing left them to spoil, but the carcases of these poor miserable creatures, wandering up and down like ghosts drawn from their graves. The smaller farms and hamlets were fortified by these robbers—English, Burgundians, Frenchmen—every one striving to do his worst. All soldiers, with one consent, plundered the farmer and the merchant. Even the cattle grew so accustomed to the alarm-bell, as the sign of an enemy's approach, that when it rung they would run home of their own accord, waiting for no guide."

And, moreover, as it has been pointed out, even greater evils than these had poor France to endure. She had lost all her principal nobility; her wealth was exhausted by long-continued war; none of her officers were equal in military capacity to the well-tried veterans of England; and her soldiers had been so often defeated by the English, that they could not be persuaded to meet them in the open field. As a natural result, England, under Henry v., had made great progress in subduing France; and when Henry v. was succeeded by his unjust son, Henry vi., the latter's Regent, John Duke of Bedford, was a bold and able general, who pursued the same victorious career as the "hero of of Agincourt." All the north of France was compelled to acknowledge the foreign king, nearly all Guienne, and the provinces belonging to the foreign king's ally, the Duke of Burgundy. The rule of Charles vii., the rightful sovereign of France, was limited to the centre and part of the south of

France, and instead of Paris, Bourges was his capital, where he lived a life of indolent ease, forgetful of the sufferings of his subjects. To make the north of France everyway their own, the English had but to capture Orleans, and though the Earl of Salisbury marched against it, the French king and his nobles showed no intention of interfering. Yet if Orleans had fallen, all France must have yielded, more or less, to the English armies, which would have proved a sore evil to both countries, the independence both of France and England being necessary, as you will learn when you grow older, to the prosperity of Europe. Orleans did *not* fall to the Earl of Salisbury, and France was *not* conquered by England; but that these two misfortunes did not occur, was by no means due to the king or the nobles of France. The glory and the honour belong to Joan of Arc.

JOAN OF ARC, JOANETTE, or JEANNE, the second daughter of Jacques d'Arc, a peasant, and Isabella Rommér, his wife, both of Domremy, a village of Vaucouleurs, on the borders of Lorraine, was born on the night of the Epiphany, 1412.

It was a pleasant country-side where Joan was born, and she grew up in health and beauty, purest among the pure, of a fine person and a sweet countenance, and gifted with an enthusiastic nature which readily yielded to the influences of religion. She was somewhat of a dreamer, too, and loved to muse by herself, wandering across the meadows, or over the green and silent hills, or by the side of the musical brook.

> "In solitude and peace
> Her soul was nurst, amidst the loveliest scenes
> Of unpolluted nature."

She was fond of story, tradition, and legend, and listened with great interest to any chronicle that told of the ancient glories of France; and among much that she learned, one thing was ever present to her memory, a prediction that France,—bleeding, unhappy France,—should be saved by a maid out of Lorraine—a maid out of the dark deep forest that was visible at the distance of three miles or so from the door of her father's cottage.

By and by she began to brood upon this strange prophecy, and upon the woes of her country, and so great was their influence on her excitable temperament, that at times she was completely carried out of herself, and it seemed to her that she heard voices from heaven addressing her. And true it is that heaven *does* speak to the devout and earnest and pure of heart, though not, indeed, exactly in the way in which the French maiden thought it spoke to *her*.

One day in the meadow, by the river-side, she was running races with her companions, for she was fleet of foot, and robust of frame, and speedily she outstripped them. She did not seem to run, but to fly, so swift was her progress over the bending grass.

"Jeanne, Jeanne," they cried, "thou art flying! thou art flying!"

Jeanne paused, triumphant, and out of breath. For a moment she turned towards the village, she listened, and then she exclaimed,

"I hear my mother call me home!"

and away she sped towards her parents' cottage.

When she arrived there, her mother inquired why she had left her sheep.

"Did you not call me?" said Jeanne; "I heard a *voice.*"

"It was not mine, child. Go back to the field."

And Jeanne returned, but it seemed to her excited fancy that she *still* heard a mysterious voice in the air.

Close by her mother's cottage was the church, with its door open daily and all day long. When Jeanne had completed her household task, she would steal into the quiet sanctuary to muse and pray. "Her books," says Miss Parr, "were the crucifix and pictures there; her learning the legends of the saints, the stories of the blessed martyrs, bits of old history and fable told over one's wheel or by the winter fire. Now and then came to Domremy a mendicant friar,[1] travel-stained and tired, seeking a night's rest and a meal, recounting the bitter distresses he had witnessed on his journeyings, opening the Gospels, his one treasure, proclaiming the good news of God, the great salvation,

---

[1] A monk who went about teaching and preaching, and lived upon the alms given to him by the devout and charitable.

the love and helpfulness of Christ to helpless men. In the pious households of the village he was always welcome, and nowhere more welcome than under the roof of Jacques d'Arc. The missionary monk scattered the good seed, and went on his way. In Jeanne's heart it struck deep root. Gifted with a rare intelligence, with an imagination pure, pious, and elevated, she began early to live a second life within her laborious actual life, a life more real and absorbing, the life of her soul, which by great powers and great sufferings was to be annealed [that is, strengthened] for a great destiny."

It is difficult to say how long it was before Jeanne's dreamy meditations shaped themselves into the firm belief that she had been chosen of God to become the saviour of France. But she affords us in her own simple narrative some clew to guide us to a decision.

"At the age of thirteen," she says, "a voice from God came nigh to me to help me in subduing myself, and that voice approached about the hour of noon, in summer time, while I lingered in my father's garden. And I had fasted the day before.

And I heard the voice on my right hand, in the direction of the church; and when I heard the voice I saw also a shining light.[1] Afterwards St. Michael, and St. Margaret, and St. Catherine appeared to me. They were encircled by a halo of glory: I saw that their brows were crowned with gems: I heard their voices, but they were soft and gentle. But I could not distinguish their arms or limbs. I heard them oftener than I saw them, and usually when the church-bells chimed for prayer. And if I went through the woods I heard them; I could clearly distinguish their voices drawing nearer and nearer to me. And when I thought I heard the celestial voices, I knelt down, and bowed my head to the very earth."

She goes on to tell us that, above all the voices, she heard one which said, "Jeanne, be thou a good child, and frequent at church; for the King of Heaven hath chosen thee to restore France." Then she fell upon her

[1] The young reader will remember that Jeanne's visions were not real; that the voice, and the light, and the figures of the saints were entirely the conception of a powerful fancy, stimulated by fasting and lonely meditation.

knees, awe-stricken, and she vowed a vow of virginity, to be kept so long as it should please God.

Nothing is more remarkable in Jeanne's career than this entire faith in her divinely-ordered mission. She clung to it to the very last. And, indeed, without this faith she could never have accomplished all she did accomplish. So the poet makes her speak of doubt as of something utterly incredible.

> "Doubt!" the Maid exclaimed,
> "It were as easy when I gaze around
> On all this fair variety of things,
> Green fields and tufted woods, and the blue depth
> Of heaven, and yonder glorious sun, to doubt
> Creating wisdom! When in the evening gale
> I breathe the mingled odours of the spring,
> And hear the wild wood melody, and hear
> The populous air vocal with insect life,
> To doubt God's goodness! There are feelings, Chief,
> Which cannot lie; and I have oftentimes
> Felt in the midnight silence of my soul
> The call of God."

Oh! my young readers, have faith in God and in yourselves,—in the work which God calls you to do,—and, believe me, your lives will ever be the purer and the happier!

For months Jeanne's excited imagination continued to hear the voices, and the visions of her solitude were constantly filled with angelic presences. Just at this time an armed force of English and Burgundians arrived to besiege Vaucouleurs, which was held for Charles VII. by Robert de Baudricourt (1420). They one day entered Domremy, and its inhabitants instantly took to flight,—some to the forest, some to distant towns for shelter. When the English and Burgundians had failed to capture Vaucouleurs, and had marched elsewhere, the villagers returned to their homes, to find them destroyed or plundered, and all their peaceful industry laid waste.

From that time Jeanne's purpose grew stronger and yet stronger. She heard the voice constantly exclaiming, "Why dost thou delay? God has great pity on the people of France. The time is come that thou must go to their deliverance." She shrunk at first from the task that seemed to be imposed upon her, but was encouraged, as she believed, by the voice of the Archangel St. Michael, and by the promise of St. Catherine and St. Margaret, her guardian saints. She grew restless and disquieted.

Her anxiety was noticed by her parents, and communicated itself to them. One morning her mother said to her, "Jeanne, thy father dreamt last night that thou wert leaving us to go away with the men-at-arms. I heard him tell thy brothers, if he believed that could happen to thee which he dreamed, he would rather see thee drowned; nay, that he would rather drown thee with his own hands."

Jeanne had ever been an obedient child; but now she felt that she could no longer obey her parents, without neglecting the great mission which, as she believed, God had imposed upon her. How was she to begin her mission seemed not the less a question very difficult to answer. The voice directed her to tell her wondrous tale to Robert de Baudricourt, Governor of Vaucouleurs; and she solicited her uncle, Durant Lavart, to conduct her to him. Durant consented, and one day, about the beginning of June, Jeanne repaired to Vaucouleurs, and began her life's work by obtaining an interview with the governor. Among others present at it, were two gentlemen of the neighbourhood, Bertrand de Poulangy and Albert d'Orontes.

Robert de Baudricourt, however, was simply a rough, gallant soldier, and he saw in Jeanne only a tall and beautiful peasant girl, possessed with some delusion about voices and angels. He listened to her story with marked incredulity, and dismissed her with the jocular advice to her uncle, that he should box her ears, and send her back to her parents. Jeanne, somewhat disheartened, returned to Domremy; but her confidence returning, and her anxiety increasing as she heard of the rapid subjugation of her country, and that the English had invested Orleans, she once more repaired to Vaucouleurs, determined to gain a second interview with the governor, and to secure his leave and license to visit the royal Court at Chinon. She tarried some time at Vaucouleurs before she gained her object. And, meantime, to those who sympathized with her, or those who ridiculed her, she constantly answered, "I must be with the Dauphin by Mid-Lent; though I should travel upon my knees I must absolutely go; the Lord wills it. It is on the part of the King of Heaven that this work is confided to me. Have you never heard how it has been prophesied that France, lost by a woman, should be restored by a maid of Lorraine?"

This prediction was generally known, and many minds were influenced in Jeanne's favour by it. Nor could they be insensible to the extraordinary enthusiasm which possessed her; and as she evidently believed in her work, so they came in time to believe in her. Her fame was noised abroad; and it was rumoured east and west, and north and south, that at Vaucouleurs was a maiden who had been specially called by God to the deliverance of France. A knight of Metz, Jean de Novelonpont, went to visit her. He was so impressed by her evident sincerity and heroic patriotism that he undertook to conduct her to the Court at Chinon, a distance of one hundred and fifty leagues. In this duty he was quickly and gladly joined by the Bertrand de Poulangy of whom we have already spoken; and Jeanne having assumed a page's dress, and mounted on a gallant horse, went forth from Vaucouleurs.

At Toul, however, Jean de Metz was compelled to leave her, and she continued her adventurous journey under the charge of her honest uncle, and of a messenger sent by Robert de Baudricourt. At Nancy she was received and kindly welcomed by the Duke of Lorraine. She then returned to Vaucouleurs for letters of introduction from the governor, and finally started on her mission on the 24th of February.

On that morning, to adopt Miss Parr's picturesque description, a company of townsfolk and country-folk, who had assembled before the governor's house, saw her come forth transformed into a young soldier, looking of the middle height of men, her luxuriant hair cut round above her ears, straight as a lance, alert, intrepid of air, of spirit, of speech. She was at this time so spare of flesh that the disguise was perfect. In the street waited, ready armed and mounted for a start, Jean de Metz and Robert de Poulangy, Count of Vienne, a king's messenger, Richard, an expert archer, a servant of the knight's, and a servant of the squire's, one of whom held the horse Jeanne was to ride. Robert de Baudricourt, who had made them all swear an oath to conduct her safely, defending her life and honour with their own until they brought her to the king, came out with her, and set her in her saddle, rallying her, meanwhile—rallying himself, perhaps—that she had made him half believe in her, begging to know whether, martial as she looked now, she ever meant to come back in peace and marry like other maidens.

"Nay, bonny Robert," she answered, "nay, it is not yet time to speak of wedded life and peaceful rest. But the Holy Spirit will provide."

The escort had now arranged themselves in due martial order, and looking round at the familiar faces from Domremy, which she had known since she was a child, and at the newer friends from Vaucouleurs who had so graciously espoused her cause, and declared their faith in her mission, Jeanne exclaimed, "Adieu! I am going into France."

"Go," answered the governor; "and let what will come of it come!" And so she rode away the Maid from Lorraine, the destined Deliverer of France; the knight, Jean de Metz, on her one hand, the squire, Bertrand de Poulangy, on the other; and as she rode, she fixed her eyes upon a golden ring, the gift of her father and mother, which was engraved with three crosses, and the words, JHESUS MARIA.

CHAPTER II.

HER DIFFICULTIES.

" Lo these the walls of Chinon, this the abode
Of Charles our monarch.   Here in revelry
He of his armies vanquish'd, his fair towns
Subdued, hears careless and prolongs the dance.
And little marvel I that to the cares
Of empire still he turns the unwilling ear,
For loss on loss, defeat upon defeat,
His strong holds taken, and his bravest Chiefs
Or slain or captured, and the hopes of youth
All blasted have subdued the royal mind
Undisciplined in Fortitude's stern school.
So may thy voice arouse his sleeping virtue !"
SOUTHEY, *Joan of Arc*, B. iii.

THE journey from Vaucouleurs to Chinon occupied eleven days, and both Jeanne and her escort were called upon to suffer many hardships. For greater safety, they travelled chiefly during the darkness, sleeping whenever and wherever they could—generally on the ground,

Jeanne wrapped in a warm woollen coverlet, but retaining her suit of armour. It was a time of the year too when the rivers and streams were dangerously swollen, but in safety Jeanne crossed the Marne above Joinville, the Aube near Bar-sur-Aube, the Seine near Bar-sur-Seine, and the Yonne at Auxerre, where she went to prayers in the cathedral.

Meantime, Orleans was almost reduced to the last extremity. It was sorely in want of provisions; the French army which had attempted to relieve it had been shamefully beaten; the English encompassed it on every side. But in this very hour of apparent hopelessness, there came on the wings of the wind "a promise and hope of miraculous deliverance, to be wrought by means of a Maid from Lorraine."

"She was coming by Gien—she was coming by Saint Catherine des Fierbois—she was coming by Chinon, where the king was —'coming to ride over the backs of the archers'—the Maid the prophet Merlin prophesied of—the Maid who was to save France, which that wicked queen, wicked woman, wicked mother, Isabeau, the she-wolf of Bavaria, had robbed from her son, and delivered into the power of the English stranger!

"Let her come! Their princes, their high priests had abandoned them, their mighty men-at-arms were nought! Let her come, the Maid from the forests of Lorraine! let her come, in the name of God, and deliver them if God would! The race was not always to the swift, nor the battle to the strong. Perchance it might please Him to show forth His power over France by the hand of this lowly maid, as he showed it of old to Israel by the hand of His servant David, the shepherd of Bethlehem, the warrior king!"

On the 6th of March, Jeanne arrived at the village of Fierbois, half-a-day's journey from Chinon; and thence she sent to the King the letter of introduction with which she had been furnished by Robert de Baudricourt. It was received with coldness and ridicule, and, for very different reasons, the King's favourite, Georges de la Tremouille, and the Archbishop of Rheims, endeavoured to prevent her from obtaining access to the King's presence. Their opposition proved ineffectual however, for the curiosity of the nation was aroused; it made itself felt in the royal council; and it was finally determined that the King should see her. In doing this, perhaps, he was influenced by a message from Dunois, the gallant defender of Orleans, who advised that her enthusiasm should be made use of; for, except in God, the city had no hope.

On the third day after her arrival at Chinon, she received a message that the King would see her. She was conducted into the royal presence by Louis de Bourbon, Count of Vendôme. "The King, to try her," says an old writer, "had taken upon him the habit of a countryman; but the Maid, being brought into the chamber, went directly to the King in this attire, and saluted him with so modest a countenance as if she had been bred up in Court all her life. They telling her that she was mistaken, she assured them it was the King, although she had never seen him.[1] She began to deliver

[1] In this there is nothing wonderful. Jeanne must have

unto him this new charge, which, she said, she had received from the God of heaven; so as she turned the eyes and minds of all men upon her."

Charles asked her what was her name.

"Jeanne the Maid," she replied.

What did she want of him?

Let us give her answer in the words of the poet:—

> "I come the appointed Minister of Heaven,
> To wield a sword before whose fated edge,
> Far, far from Orleans shall the English wolves
> Speed their disastrous flight. Monarch of France!
> Send thou the tidings over all the realm,
> Great tidings of deliverance and of joy;
> The Maid is come, the mission'd Maid, whose hand
> Shall in the consecrated walls of Rheims
> Crown thee, anointed King."

The courtiers were inclined to laugh at the idea of a royal progress to Rheims, then the very centre of the power of England and Burgundy. But Charles drew the Maid aside, and held secret converse with her. She gratified the Dauphin's mind (for he was

heard frequent descriptions of the person and countenance of the King, and would also, with her quick eye, detect his naturally royal bearing.

not yet king), by assuring him that he was —what in his heart he had doubted—the legitimate and rightful heir to the throne of France ; and he conceived a great confidence in her.

Yet it was some time before he and his counsellors could decide upon the employment of her services. Most of them seemed to have believed that she was inspired, but could not satisfy themselves whether the inspiration came from good or evil spirits. As if there would be thought of ill in that pure heart, so wholly devoted to its God and country! At length it was resolved that she should be closely questioned by a commission of ecclesiastics, and of professors from the great law-school of Poitiers. Strong in her simplicity and innocence she stood before these learned doctors, and related the story of her life, and satisfied all their questions. Thus, one of them suggested that if God were willing to deliver the people of France out of their calamities, He would deliver them without the assistance of men-at-arms.

Jeanne's reply was admirable :

"The men-at-arms," she said, "must fight, and God would give the victory."

The commission wisely reported to the King that he might lawfully avail himself of the Maid's services, since they had discovered in her nothing but what should be in a good Christian and good Catholic.

Various other inquiries having been made, the King issued the following proclamation, which was enthusiastically received in every part of France:—

"The King, seeing the necessity of his kingdom, and considering the prayers of his poor people, ought not to reject the Maid, who says she is sent of God to succour him, even though her promises be but human works, neither ought he lightly to receive her. But, following Holy Writ, he ought to prove her in two ways,—by human prudence, inquiring into her life, behaviour, and intention; and by devout prayer, asking a sign whether she be come by the will of God or not, as Hezekiah, Gideon, and others also asked.

"The King, since the coming of the Maid, has thus sought to prove her, keeping her near him for six weeks, and causing her birth, her life, her conduct, and her intentions to be inquired into by all manner of people—scholars, churchmen, men of piety, men of war, wives, widows, and others. Publicly and privately she has conversed with them, and none find in her any evil, but only chastity, humility, devotion, simplicity, and honour; and of her birth and life many marvellous things are told for true.

"As to the second means of proving her, the King has received a sign of her, to which she replies, that before the city of Orleans she will show him a sign, and not elsewhere, for so God has commanded her.

"Having regard to this, that no harm is found in her, that she promises a sign before Orleans, considering her constancy and perseverance in her purpose, and her urgent plea that she may go to Orleans with men-at-arms, the King ought not to hold her back, but to let her be conducted thither honourably, hoping in God. For to doubt her, and set her aside without any appearance of evil, would be to do despite to the

Holy Spirit of Grace, and to render himself unworthy of the succour of God."

Jeanne was now provided, by the royal order, with all the pomp and circumstance of a military commander. She was attired in a suit of armour of spotless white. A black charger of matchless beauty was set apart for her use. In her right hand she carried a lance, which she had learned to wield with admirable skill; at her side hung a small battle-axe, and the consecrated sword which, as the Voices had revealed to her, lay buried behind the altar in the church of St. Catherine de Fierbois. She requested that it might be sent for, and, in the place she described, it was surely found. This mysterious sword, whose blade was engraved with five crosses, was placed by the priest in a scabbard of crimson velvet. The citizens of Tours provided a sword scabbard made of cloth-of-gold, but Jeanne herself, knowing what was best fitted for actual work, ordered a scabbard of leather.

She wore no helmet on her brow, which was simply crowned with a wreath of amber hair, and thus the fire and lustre of her eyes were manifest to every beholder. A page carried her banner, which had been woven in obedience to the direction of the Heavenly Voices. The white satin folds of white satin were strewn with fleurs-de-lis, and bore a representation of the Saviour in His glory, and the words IHESUS MARIA. This consecrated banner was dearer to the Maid than sword, or axe, or spear, for, with a true woman's feeling, she shrunk from the use of a deadly weapon.

It is not to be wondered at that her appearance among the soldiers of France should arouse in them a new spirit. Her chivalrous bearing, her beautiful and animated countenance, and the skill with which she managed her steed, increased the emotion already awakened by the reports of her divine mission. "A new spirit was breathed through the once despondent ranks. The rigid discipline she enjoined added to the general effect. She drove from the camp its usual profligate followers." She insisted that both officers and men should attend the public services of the Church. At every halting-place she caused an altar to be erected, and the sacrament administered. Oaths and unclean language were severely punished. All excess was forbidden. "The French army felt the impulse of a pure and holy influence, and marched forward under the very Shadow of the Cross, saints as well as warriors, led, as they believed, by no mere woman, by no Virgin only, however gentle and fair, but by an Angel from heaven, whose task it was to deliver France from the oppression of her foes."

It is thus that the conviction of the one becomes the enthusiasm of the many, and that a devout spirit of earnestness gains uncontrolled power over the minds of men.

CHAPTER III.

VICTORY.

"Lo! where the holy banner waved aloft,
　The lambent lightnings play. Irradiate round,
　As with a blaze of glory, o'er the field
　It stream'd miraculous splendour. Then their hearts
　Sunk, and the English trembled. . . .
　　　　　　　　　Swift they fled
　From that portentous banner, and the sword
　Of France; though Talbot with vain valiancy
　Yet urged the war, and stemm'd alone the tide
　Of battle. Even their leaders felt dismay;
　Fastolffe fled first, and Salisbury in the rout
　Mingled, and all impatient of defeat,
　Borne backward Talbot turns. Then echoed loud
　The cry of conquest, deeper grew the storm,
　And darkness, hovering o'er on raven wing,
　Brooded the field of death."
　　　　　　　　SOUTHEY, *Joan of Arc*, B. vi.

WHILE we have the Maid marching towards Orleans, we must carry our young readers thither to show them the position of the English army, and the condition of the city.

The English forces, under the leadership of the gallant and able Earl of Salisbury, appeared before the walls of Orleans on the 12th of October 1428. This fair historic city, as a modern writer tells us, clusters upon the northern bank of the Loire, encircled by smiling plains and productive vineyards. Its inhabitants, at the time we speak of, were men of an heroic and patriotic spirit, fully conscious of the responsibility enjoined upon them, fully conscious that on the fate of Orleans depended the fate of France. Therefore they had made, and up to the last continued to make, every preparation for a resolute defence. They cleared away all the houses in its suburbs down to the very margin of the river; they levelled all the splendid chateaux or mansions which reared their turrets among the surrounding groves; and they accumulated ample supplies of food, arms, and ammunition. Then, when the English pushed forward their attack, they hurled upon them shot, and javelins, and arrows; fighting as gallantly as it was possible for men to do. Then the besiegers, protecting themselves as they advanced by throwing up rude banks of earth, continued to push nearer and nearer to the city; and as they pushed forward, they connected all their works, until on the north the city was completely invested.

On the south, Orleans was connected with the north bank of the river by a strong fortified bridge, defended by two towers, called the Tourelles, which were built on the bridge itself, just at the point where it rested on a little island. In fact the solid masonry or stonework of the bridge terminated at these Tourelles, and a drawbridge extended from thence to the southern shore. Meantime, at the head of the bridge was a small fort of the kind which the French call *tête du pont*, and this, in conjunction with the Tourelles, created a really formidable outwork, capable of holding a large garrison, and enabling the Orleannais—the inhabitants of Orleans—to go forth under its shelter and obtain all kinds of supplies and reinforcements from the southern provinces.

I think you will understand from this description that the Tourelles were a very important point. You see, reader, that on the north the city lies shut in by the English entrenchments, and from that side could obtain no food or stores. But this did not seriously matter, so long as communication with the outer country could be secured through the Tourelles; and hence the English commanders saw that the city would not surrender until the Tourelles were captured. Against the Tourelles therefore, the Earl of Salisbury directed his most earnest efforts, and after several severe repulses, he carried it by assault on the 23d October. Strange to say, his success, which seemed to promise complete victory to the English arms, was destined to be the cause of their ultimate disgrace and failure. On one occasion the Earl had ascended one of the Tourelles, and from the higher windows was surveying the defensive works of the town, when he was struck by a stone shot fired from an enemy's cannon, and so severely wounded that within eight days he died. A terrible loss was this to our English army, for his successor in the command had neither his military genius, his experience, or his influence over his soldiery. Well may Shakespeare exclaim :—

> "Accursèd tower, accursèd fatal hand
> That hath contrived this woful tragedy.
> In thirteen battles Salisbury o'ercame;
> Henry the Fifth he first trained to the wars;
> Whilst any trump did sound, or drum struck up,
> His sword did ne'er leave striking in the field."

The city was now completely swept by the English foe, and all the exertions of the famous Dunois, who guided the defence, could do nothing but delay for awhile the fatal hour of surrender. But it was evident that famine and suffering would soon compel even *him* to submit.

The English themselves were not wholly exempt from the pangs of hunger, until relieved by the victory which Sir John Fastolfe gained over the enemy at Rouvrai, near Orleans, towards the middle of March, 1429. In this brilliant action the superior courage of the English seemed conclusively proved by their defeat of 4000 French and Scots with only 1600 fighting men. This achievement cleared the surrounding country of the enemy's scattered forces, and large convoys of food and ammunition reached the Earl of Suffolk's camp in safety.[1] Never, says a writer, never had the spirit of the invaders risen so high, and never had the fortunes of France fallen so low. The inhabitants were on the brink of submission to the English, when Jeanne of Arc made her appearance upon the scene, and, "as on the mimic stage the waving wand of the enchanter will suddenly transform the devastation of winter into the bloom and verdure and fresh young beauty of the spring," so her presence awoke hope where despondency had prevailed, and insured victory where ruin had seemed inevitable.

With a small French army, brought together from various points, Jeanne the Maid set out for Orleans on the 25th of April. She was accompanied by Dunois, who had made his escape from the besieged city to carry the sad tidings of its condition to

---

[1] Owing to the circumstance that this convoy was largely composed of salt fish for the Lenten repasts of the English soldiers, the engagement referred to above was popularly called the "Battle of the Herrings."

Charles at Chinon. On the 20th, they approached the town; where,

> "Embosomed in the depth
> Of that old forest, which for many a league
> Shadow'd the hills and vales of Orleannois,
> They pitch their tents. The hum of occupation
> Sounds ceaseless. Waving to the evening gale
> The streamers flutter; and ascending slow
> Beneath the foliage of the forest trees,
> With many a light hue tinged, the curling smoke
> Melts in the impurpled air."

Next day, or rather next night, in a great storm of rain and thunder, the Maid, with her knights and men-at-arms, her provisions and artillery, entered the city,[1] and on the following morning she passed through all its streets, clad in her brilliant armour, and mounted on a snow-white steed. Each person who gazed upon her felt himself the better, and braver, and purer for the sight. It was as if an angel had come down from heaven, and inspired them with celestial spirit.

When it was known that the Maid—ap-

---

[1] The English had been rendered over-confident of success, or they might easily have checked her course, and in so doing abruptly terminated her career.

parently by a miracle—had broken through their lines, the English were sorely amazed. With all the credulity of the time, they believed the wonderful stories reported of her; but instead of deeming her to be an angel from above, they considered her the special and favoured servant of the Evil One. They were a superstitiously pious soldiery, says Miss Parr; they were assured that they did well in taking away the dominion of France from her false and cruel princes; they had been so long prosperous, that it was impossible for them to conceive of God going over to the other side. When, therefore, terror fell upon them, with defeat, humiliation, grievous destruction, they referred all their calamities to Satanic agency; and as the Satan of the middle ages was a very real and practical power among men, they gave way before him, supposing that he was to reign for a season, and that their turn and God's would come again by and by.

Now that the Maid had entered Orleans, she lost no time in attempting its relief. She despatched heralds to the English commander, bidding them surrender to her, the messenger of Heaven, the keys of the French cities which they had unjustly seized, and ordering them to retire from Orleans. The English threatened to burn her heralds. Then she mounted one of the ramparts of the town, within hearing of the Tourelles, and, with her own voice, repeated her message. The English garrison at this important post was commanded by a rude but able captain, Sir William Gladsdale, or, as Jeanne called him, Glacidas. He was afraid neither of men nor of witches, and he replied to Jeanne with coarse mouth, bidding her go home and milk her cows. Unfortunately the common soldiers did not show the incredulity of their commanders; and it was evident that the warriors who had never turned their backs to a foe, or quailed before the greatest odds, were now panic-stricken by the appearance of a simple woman—a young fair girl—because they had invested her with supernatural powers.

A day or two afterwards, Dunois, to whom and his fellow-knights the Maid wisely left the direction of every military movement, seized upon what seemed a favourable occasion to attack the English fort, and was met with a gallant resistance. Jeanne was resting at home, when suddenly, as she afterwards declared, the *Voices* informed her of what was going on, and, calling for her lance, she hastily donned her suit of radiant armour, mounted her horse, and proceeded to join in the battle. In her haste she had forgotten her banner. She rode back for it, and to prevent her dismounting, it was handed to her from the windows of her lodgings. Then she galloped hastily to the gate from which the French had issued to the attack, meeting on her way with some of the Orleannais returning wounded. "Ha!" she cried, "I am aware no French blood flows without my hair standing upon end!" As soon as she came up with the main body of the retreating troops, she rallied them with words of hearty encouragement; waving her banner, she placed herself at their head, and assuring them of victory, led them back to the assault.

The English fell into a panic at the sight of the beautiful Maid, whom they supposed to be a sorceress. Their tried courage suddenly gave way; St. Loup was carried by storm, and its defenders put to the sword, except some few whom Jeanne tenderly rescued. For though she knew blood must be shed, she was averse to shedding it, and her tears flowed freely when she saw around her a heap of the dead and dying; many of whom, she reflected, must have passed to their last account without a sigh of repentance or a prayer for forgiveness.

The next day, the Feast of the Ascension, kept in the Romish as in the English Church with due solemnity, was devoted to the service of God. On the following, the besieged, who were now equal or perhaps superior in power to the besiegers, made a desperate sally against the English forts on the south of the river. The French crossed the Loire in boats; mounted the walls in a phrenzy of fierce enthusiasm, and after a fierce hand-to-hand fight, captured the English "bastiles," as they were then called, of the Augustine and St. Jean de Blanc, leaving only the important fort of the Tourelles untaken. In this encounter Jeanne was wounded in the heel.

The great military value of the Tourelles was known both to French and English, for it commanded the town and the channel of communication with the country beyond. The Duke of Bedford, then acting as Regent of France for Henry VI., had despatched a strong reinforcement to the English, to strengthen them against the increased numbers of the French; and the latter felt that it was urgently necessary to attack the Tourelles before this reinforcement arrived, and while the presence of the Maid still awakened in them the inspiration of enthusiasm. Dunois, their leader, was too able a commander not to be aware of the difficulty of the enterprise. He knew that the ramparts and defensive works of the Tourelles were of a formidable character, and that they were garrisoned by 800 men, the flower of the English army, under the leadership of a veteran captain, Sir John Gladsdale.

Early on the morning of the 7th of May, the bells were rung, and mass in every church was sung, by order of the Maid; and the French soldiers having performed their usual devotions, but with more than usual fervour, were carried across the Loire in boats, and led to the attack. Both sides displayed an equal valour; but, for once, the French fought with unflinching tenacity—a quality in which they have generally shown themselves deficient. And why? Because the presence and example of the Maid inspired them. Waving her banner, she rode in amongst their ranks, cheering them with words of hope, and promises of triumph. " She rallied the flying, she spurred the laggard, was herself most conspicuous wherever danger was most imminent. To and fro in the storm of fire along the shore, where flash answered to flash, and thunder to thunder, where through the volleying clouds of smoke whistled the shrill arrows sowing the bloody plain with death, went she, calm, valiant, beautiful, constant, strong, untiring."

Battle-axes were swung lustily, and swords rung against crest and breast, when Jeanne, seizing a ladder, was the first to gain the rampart. Just as she was on the point of mounting it, an arrow whistled through the air, and wounded her smartly between the neck and shoulder. But before the English could leap from the battlement and make her prisoner, she was borne away to the rear. Laid upon the grass, and her cuirass removed, with the agony of her wound she began to weep; for, like a true woman, she was prone to tears. But, raising herself as if by some sudden inspiration from heaven, she sat up, drew the arrow from the wound with her own hands, and having dressed it with a little oil, betook herself to prayer.

After a while she resumed her armour, and returned to the fray, when the enthusiasm of the French had begun to wane, and the courage of the English seemed so invincible that Dunois and his captains debated on the advisability of retreat.

The Maid's quick eye, however, had noticed that the English were nearly spent with the fatigue of their resistance against so large a host. Their firing was losing its skill and force: a man, she said, would have thrown a ball with his hand, with as much force as their guns; let the French eat, and drink, and rest themselves; and then, returning to the assault, they could not fail to be victorious.

So, when the soldiers had taken their refreshment, she addressed them with all her fire and spirit. "Return," she exclaimed, "in the name of God, return to the attack once more! The English are exhausted, and can no longer defend themselves. Go in against them boldly, and both the rampart and the Tourelles shall be yours."

Seizing her banner, she rushed to the brink of the fosse or moat, shouting aloud : "Surrender, Gladsdale, surrender to the King of Heaven! Foul wrong didst thou do me with thy speech, but I take great pity on thy soul and on the souls of thy men!" Onward went the holy banner towards the fort. The English on the rampart, weary and exhausted, were seized with a sudden fear. They could not understand the courage of this fair and lovely maiden, unless, indeed, she were assisted by supernatural powers; and if so, who would prevail against her? Jeanne detected their dismay. "Go, children, in God's name!" she cried, "and they are ours!" And the French swarmed over the walls, and carried the ramparts.

Gladsdale, accompanied by some thirty knights and men, fled to the Tourelles. They crossed the drawbridge in safety, but just as they reached the stone arch, it was struck by a heavy cannon-shot, gave way with a crash, and precipitated them all into the Loire. The weight of their armour prevented them from swimming, and they sunk immediately. At their terrible fate Jeanne uttered a sigh of pity, then gave way to her womanly feelings, and burst into bitter tears. But the battle was won. A few planks were thrown across the broken arch, and the French pressed across them to the assault of the Tourelles. It was now six o'clock, and the English acknowledged their defeat. Not one Englishman was left on the south bank of the Loire. Those who were not killed or drowned were led prisoners into Orleans. So terrible, so overwhelming was the reverse of fortune!

It is strange that Suffolk and Talbot, who had watched the whole day's battle from some of their northern forts, had made no attempt to relieve the Tourelles, or to attack the almost unguarded city. Either they were incompetent generals, though brave men; or they were stunned and surprised by this novel enthusiasm of the French; or they found themselves helpless because their men would not fight against witchcraft.

The capture of the Tourelles was unquestionably a splendid achievement; and well might a grateful people fill the air with shouts of "Glory to God and the Maid!" She had promised to return into Orleans across the bridge. There were enough, and to spare, of willing hands ready to repair its breaches, that she might pass over it safely, and fulfil her promise. And as she entered the city, the bells rang out from every spire and tower; the streets kindled into a blaze of light; and the Orleannais rejoiced like men who have been saved from a fiery furnace. And, on the following morning, when they assembled on their walls, and gathered along the river-bank, they saw that the English had set on fire their forts, and were retiring from Orleans, in admirable order, but in sullen discontent. They drew up in full battle array, as if inviting the French to try their fortune in the open field. But, "In the name of God," said Jeanne, "let them go, and let us return thanks to the Lord! We will not pursue them, nor kill them; for to-day is Sunday!"

After this prosaic description, it may well be that our readers will find a pleasure in perusing some of the animated passages in which the poet Southey tells the story of the deliverance of Orleans; and, first, for the incident of Jeanne's wound:—

> "Burning at the sight
> With indignation, Glacidas[1] beheld
> His troops fly scatter'd; fast on every side
> The foe up-rushing eager to their spoil;
> The holy standard waving; and the Maid
> Fierce in pursuit. 'Speed but this arrow, Heaven!'
> The chief exclaim'd, 'and I shall fall content.'
> So saying, he his sharpest quarrel[2] chose,
> And fix'd the bow-string, and against the Maid
> Levelling, let loose: her arm was raised on high
> To smite a fugitive; he glanced aside,
> Shunning her deadly stroke, and thus received
> The chieftain's arrow: through his ribs it pass'd,
> And cleft that vessel whence the purer blood
> Through many a branching channel o'er the frame
> Meanders.

---

[1] That is, Gladsdale. The details here introduced are, of course, fictitious.   [2] An arrow.

> 'Fool!' the exasperate Knight exclaim'd,
> 'Would she had slain thee! thou hast lived too long.'
> Again he aim'd his arbalist: the string
> Struck forceful: swift the erring arrow sped
> Guiltless of blood, for lightly o'er the court
> Bounded the warrior Virgin. Glacidas
> Levell'd his bow again! the fated shaft
> Fled true, and difficultly through the mail
> Pierced to her neck, and tinged its point with blood.
> 'She bleeds! she bleeds!' exulting cried the chief;
> 'The sorceress bleeds! nor all her hellish arts
> Can charm my arrows from their destined course.'
> Ill-fated man! in vain with eager hand
> Placing thy feather'd quarrel in its groove,
> Dream'st thou of Joan subdued! She from her neck
> Plucking the shaft unterrified, exclaim'd,
> 'This is a favour! Frenchmen, let us on!
> Escape they cannot from the hand of God!'"[1]

The retreat of the English is thus narrated:—

> "The English chiefs . . . counselling
> They met despondent. Suffolk, now their chief,
> Since Salisbury fell, began.
>   'It now were vain
> Lightly of this our more than mortal foe
> To speak contemptuous. She hath vanquish'd us,
> Aided by Hell's leagued powers, nor aught avails
> Man unassisted 'gainst Infernal powers
> To dare the conflict. Were it best remain
> Waiting the doubtful aid of Burgundy,
> Doubtful and still delay'd? or from this place,
> Scene of our shame, retreating as we may,

---

[1] According to the historian Hall, these were actually Jeanne's words.

Yet struggle to preserve the guarded towns
Of the Orleannois!'
                    He ceased, and with a sigh,
Struggling with pride that heaved his gloomy breast,
Talbot replied, 'Our council little boots;
For by their numbers now made bold in fear
The soldiers will not fight, they will not heed
Our vain resolves, heart-wither'd by the spells
Of this accursed sorceress. Soon will come
The expected host from England; even now
Perchance the tall bark scuds across the deep
That bears my son: young Talbot comes, . . he comes
To find his sire disgraced! But soon mine arm,
By vengeance nerved, and shame of such defeat,
Shall from the crest-fall'n courage of yon witch,
Regain its ancient glory. Near the coast
Best is it to retreat, and there expect
The coming succour.'
                    Thus the warrior spake.
Joy ran through all the troops, as though retreat
Were safety. Silently in order'd ranks
They issue forth, favour'd by the thick clouds
Which mantled o'er the moon. With throbbing hearts
Fearful they speeded on; some in sad thoughts
Of distant England, and now wise too late,
Cursing in bitterness the evil hour
That led them from her shores; some in faint hope
Thinking to see their native land again;
Talbot went musing on his former fame
Sullen and stern, and feeding on dark thoughts,
And meditating vengeance."

Thus on the 8th of May, the tenth day after the Maid's arrival at Orleans, the siege was raised, and the first step taken towards the severance of France from England; a blessed result for both nations, and for civilisation at large.

It was the Maid's wish to celebrate so glorious a success, due, as she believed, to the direct interposition of Providence, by a solemn religious ceremony in the Cathedral. An immense crowd of knights, and men-at-arms, and citizens assembled. High mass was celebrated, a *Te Deum* sung, and a sermon preached.

Afterwards, they all gathered in a solemn procession, each one bearing a lighted taper, and the monks and priests at their head. They slowly moved around the delivered city, and prayers were said and praises sung in all the places where the English had formerly established their works.

"*Antiphony*.[1]—Our enemies are gathered together, and boast themselves in their strength. Lord, bring to nought their strength, and scatter them; for there is none other that fighteth for us, but only Thou, O God.

[1] Antiphony,—that is, alternate singing: first, one set of voices, then another.

"Abase their pride, and lower their presumption.

"Drive them hither and thither, and carry them utterly away.

"Lord, hear our prayer.

"And let our cry come unto Thee.

"*Let us pray.*

"O God, the Author of Peace, who without bow and arrow can expel the enemies of those who hope in Thee, come to our help; be favourable to us in our adversity; and inasmuch as Thou hast delivered Thy people by the hand of a woman, so, for Charles our king, lift up the arm of victory, that the foe, who trust in the multitude of their archers, and glorify themselves in their spearmen, may presently be overcome; and to Thee, who art the way, the truth, and the life, all the people shall give praise, for our Lord Jesus Christ's sake. Amen."

And to this day the anniversary of the deliverance of Orleans is solemnly observed by its citizens.

CHAPTER IV.

DIFFICULTIES.

"The morn was fair
When Rheims re-echoed to the busy hum
Of multitudes, for high solemnity
Assembled. To the holy fabric moves
The long procession, through the streets bestrewn
With flowers and laurel boughs. . . .

"By the king
The delegated Damsel pass'd along
Clad in her batter'd arms. She bore on high
Her hallow'd banner to the sacred pile,
And fix'd it on the altar, whilst her hand
Pour'd on the monarch's head the mystic oil. . . .

"The mission'd Maid
Then placed on Charles's brow the crown of France,
And back retiring, gazed upon the king
One moment, quickly scanning all the past,
Till in a tumult of wild wonderment
She wept aloud."—SOUTHEY, *Joan of Arc* B. x.

THE glad tidings of the relief of Orleans was conveyed to Charles on the 10th of May, and he immediately announced the all-important fact in a public proclamation. "More than ever," it said, "ought we to thank our Creator, who, of His Divine clemency, has not left us in forgetfulness; and we cannot enough honour the virtuous and marvellous deeds which are reported to us of the Maid, who was always present in person at the execution of these things."

Jeanne now quitted the delivered city, and proceeded to Blois, and from thence to Tours, being everywhere received with the welcome due to conquerors and heroes. At Tours she was duly honoured by the King; but Charles was, unhappily, a man of fickle disposition, and he soon turned aside to listen to the sneers, and follow the advice, of his unworthy favourites.

The English, meantime, were protesting loudly that Jeanne was a witch, a sorceress, prompted by evil spirits, under the rule of the devil; and we doubt not that in their shame at their defeat, and in their amazement at her courage, they *did* truly and really believe in her supernatural powers. Yet her only magic was that of enthusiasm, and her only helping spirits were her own innocence and constancy.

Jeanne's advice to the King was, that he should instantly proceed to Rheims, and be publicly crowned. She rightly judged that by this act he would be declaring himself lawful king of France, and that its effect on the popular mind would be most beneficial. But the royal councillors were both less sagacious and less hurried; they advised that the English should first be swept from the valley of the Loire. But while they hesitated, the army which had been got together for the relief of Orleans rapidly dissolved, and it was some weeks before another could be assembled.

Charles retired to the castle of Loches, whither he was accompanied by Jeanne d'Arc. She soon grew weary of inaction, and again besought the Dauphin to repair to Rheims, declaring that, after his coronation, the power of his enemies would go to decay, and they would do little more injury to his kingdom. "Noble Dauphin," she said, "do not hold so many or such tedious councils, but come quickly to the city of Rheims and receive your crown."

One of the officials present asked her, if her *counsel* (as she sometimes called it) had bidden her to act thus. She said that such was the case, and that it continually urged her to carry on the work that was given her to do.

"Will you tell us here," he said, "here, in the King's presence, in what manner your *counsel* speaks when it talks with you?"

Jeanne blushed, and answered him emphatically, "In my own mind I conceive what you wish to know, and I will tell you."

The King, courteously interrupting her, said :—" Jeanne, are you willing to declare it before these witnesses?"

She said that she would do so gladly, and proceeded to tell them that when she was unhappy, ready belief was not given to her messages on the part of God. She went aside, and lamented to Him that they to whom she conveyed them were so unwilling to put faith in them. And after she had made her prayer, she always heard a voice saying to her: "Go on, daughter of God; I will be with thee to help thee; go on, go on." She added that, when she heard the voice, she was inexpressibly happy, and would wish ever to continue in that state. And in repeating the words of her *counsel*, she lifted up her eyes to heaven with an ecstasy which, it is said, none of the witnesses ever forgot.

But Charles and his councillors, however much impressed at the time, quickly got rid of the impression, and Jeanne was compelled to be content with the King's promise that, when the country round about Orleans had been swept of the English, he would proceed to Rheims. An army was therefore assembled under the command of the Duke of Alençon, with the view of expelling the English from the fortified towns of Jergeau, Meun, Beaugency, and Yenville. Orleans was made their rendezvous, and from Orleans they set out, accompanied by the Maid, twelve hundred lances strong, besides common foot-soldiers, all filled with the utmost confidence in the success of their expedition.

The first town they besieged was Jergeau; and the incidents of its siege are so graphically told by Miss Harriet Parr, that instead of resorting to the crabbed style of the old chronicles, we shall adopt the modern historian's more elegant language:—

The Maid summoned Suffolk and the English garrison in her usual style: "Surrender the town to the King of Heaven and King Charles, and go your way, or evil will befall you." Suffolk desired to treat, and asked for a truce of fifteen days. This the French captains would not grant, but they proposed to let him and his men march out with arms and horses, if they would march at once. Here, however, the Maid raised her voice, saying: "They shall save their lives only, and begone in their smocks, or I will have them by assault." Suffolk despised and refused her terms, and the bombards, cannon, and culverins were brought up under cover of night, and placed in position against the ramparts.

The firing opened at dawn, and all that day and the next night passed in attacks, sallies, and repulses. The walls were then much battered, and about nine o'clock on Monday morning the trumpets sounded, and the heralds cried, "To the assault!"

Foremost came the Maid, sweeping gaily down towards the fosse, with her standard displayed, and calling to the Duke of Alençon, "Forward, gentle Duke, to the assault!" Alençon had not given the command, and, considering it premature, he told her so. Jeanne answered him, undaunted: "Never doubt! The hour is when it pleases God. We must work when He wills. Work now, and He will work with us."

Alençon still demurred and hung back, on which she said, laughing and mocking at him: "Ah, gentle Duke, art thou afraid? Dost thou not know that I have promised thy wife to send thee back to her safe and sound?"

He advanced with her then, and the assault began. The defence was courageous and steady for nearly four hours; the attack was as fierce and persistent. Master Jean, a gunner from Orleans, did his duty ably, and "picked off" with his recovered culverin a tall Englishman, whom Alençon pointed out as a very galling annoyance to the assailants. The Maid had a far and clear sight, and once she warned the Duke out of danger, telling him that if he did not change his position, there was a piece on the walls would do him a damage. He moved aside, and the next moment a gentleman of Anjou, stepping into his place, was killed.

At the time and the point when the assault was hottest, and the resistance most desperate, the Maid descended into the fosse, bearing her standard and encouraging her men by word and art. She had set her foot on a ladder to scale the rampart herself, when an English soldier cast down upon her from above a large stone which struck her standard, and rebounding on her steel cap, flung her to the ground. The stone itself was dashed to fragments; but in an instant Jeanne was up again, crying: " Friends, friends, cheer up! cheer up! Our Lord has condemned the English. This day they are ours. Be of good heart! Come on! come on!"

The men, invoked to fresh enthusiasm by

her invincible spirit, rushed forward impetuously. Suffolk, from the ramparts, shouted out for speech with the Duke of Alençon. He was not heeded. The assault was furiously pressed, and the English, unable any longer to defend the wall, endeavoured to escape over the bridge into the castle. But the French followed hard after them. One Guillaume Regnault laid his hand on the Earl of Suffolk, summoning him to yield himself a prisoner. Suffolk asked his captor if he was a gentleman, and when Regnault had satisfied him of that, he asked if he was a knight. Regnault said he had not yet attained that honour. "Then I make you one," replied the Earl; and before giving up his sword to the young soldier, he dubbed him one of the brotherhood of chivalry. With Suffolk was taken his brother John. His brother Alexander was slain, and in the pursuit through the streets of the town there perished more than five hundred men.

Such is Miss Parr's account of the siege and capture of Jergeau. Our readers will wonder, doubtless, how a woman so fair, so gentle, and so tender as the Maid could mingle in these scenes of bloodshed. But we must remember that when any one of us has a particular work to do, we must do that work, however hard and disagreeable it may be to us. Jeanne's work was to deliver France from our ancestors, who, brave and chivalrous as they were, were also fond of conquest and military glory, and had no more right to conquer France than the French would have had to conquer England. Such a task could not be accomplished, alas! without much loss of life; but it is noticeable that Jeanne never slew or wounded any man with her own hand, and more generally carried her banner than either sword or spear.

The fate of Jergeau taught the garrisons of Beaugency and Meun that submission was the first policy; and Talbot, who had now succeeded to the English command, and of whom Shakespeare has made so heroic a character, gathered into one body the remaining English troops, and retreated hastily towards the Seine. As he retired he was met by Sir John Fastolfe with a reinforce-

DIFFICULTIES. 63

ment of 4000 men. At the same time, the French chieftains received an almost equal accession of force under Arthur de Richemont, the Lord Constable of France. He had long been on ill terms with the King; or, rather, the King with him, and Jeanne, whose loyalty was enthusiastic, proposed to go forth, and give him battle. But such a proposal naturally excited great dissatisfaction, and Jeanne was at length brought to understand that civil discord—that war between two parties of the same country—was by no means a successful means of expelling their common enemy. Union is strength!

She therefore agreed to welcome the Constable in his taking an oath of loyalty, and to use her influence with the King to have his faults forgiven.

The combined forces then pushed forward with the view of overtaking the English army in its retreat. On the 18th of June they came up with it near the village of Patay. But the English were Englishmen no longer. They would fight the French, it is true, but they could not fight that one modest woman, whom, in their ignorance, they regarded as the creature of Satan.[1] They scarcely kept their ranks a moment. The battle was won before it was fought. Even the gallant Fastolfe fled at the first fire; in punishment for which act of cowardice he was afterwards expelled from the Order of the Garter. Talbot, indeed, disdained to show his back to an enemy: he dismounted, and fought on foot among the foremost, but, being left almost alone, he was speedily taken prisoner; while upwards of 2000 men were killed in the pursuit.

[1] The common belief that Jeanne was aided by spells and witchcraft, and could command the services of fiends, is perpetuated by Shakespeare in his *Henry VI.*, Part I. Act v. sc. 3, where the Maid, or La Pucelle, is represented as summoning her spirits to help her:—

"The regent conquers, and the Frenchmen fly.
  Now, help, ye charming spells, and periapts;
  And ye choice spirits that admonish me,
  And give me signs of future accidents!   [*Thunder.*
  You speedy helpers, that are substitutes
  Under the lordly monarch of the north,
  Appear, and aid me in this enterprise!
                        [*Enter Fiends.*
This speedy and quick appearance argues proof
Of your accustomed diligence to me.
Now, ye familiar spirits, that are cull'd
Out of the powerful regions under earth,
Help me this once, that France may get the field."

DIFFICULTIES.

After this signal victory, Charles could no longer refuse Jeanne's urgent request that he would proceed to Rheims for his coronation. Such an expedition, as Earl Stanhope remarks, was still overcast by doubts and perils. Rheims itself, and every other city on the way, was in the hands of enemies; and a superior force, either of English from the left, or of Burgundians from the right, might assail the advancing army.

These difficulties were increased by Charles himself, who, at this time of his life, shrank from any special exertion. Nevertheless the enthusiasm of his troops was so great, and her influence so all-powerful, that he could no longer refuse.

Assembling at Gien a force of from ten to twelve thousand men, he marched from the valley of the Loire, accompanied by Jeanne herself, by his ablest councillors and bravest captains. On appearing before Auxerre they obtained a supply of provisions. Troyes was defended by a garrison of 500 Burgundian soldiers, and it held out for some days; but the great renown of the Maid here too won a victory, and the citizens threw wide their gates, and loyally acknowledged Charles to be their king.

This new-born loyalty spread onwards to Châlons and to Rheims. In each city the inhabitants expelled the Burgundian garrisons, and proclaimed King Charles.

And then it came to pass that on the early morning of Saturday, the 16th of July, the great object of Jeanne's mission was accomplished, and, attended by princes, and knights, and great lords, with an immense crowd of citizens and peasants following and surrounding him, Charles entered Rheims. And among that crowd stood Jeanne's father, who had come from Domremy, with her brother Pierre, to rejoice in this wonderful and unexpected triumph. The meeting between them was very tender, and proved that no series of successes, no blaze of renown, could weaken the gentle Maid's domestic affections.

On the day following, Sunday the 17th, the coronation of King Charles took place.

The ceremonial began at nine in the morning, and did not terminate until two in the afternoon. Three hundred knights and gentlemen were present at it, and every rite was celebrated with the utmost splendour and formality. Next the altar, bearing her holy banner, stood the Maid, "to whom, after God, were all thanks due for bringing King Charles's sacred coronation to pass." She was afterwards asked at her trial, "Why was your banner thus honoured beyond all other banners?" "It had shared the danger," she replied, "and it had a right to share the glory."

The functions of the spiritual peers were performed by the Archbishop of Rheims, the Bishops of Châlons, Orleans, and Seiz, and two others whose names are not recorded. The leading lay peers present were the Dukes of Burgundy, Normandy, and Aquitaine, and the Counts of Flanders, Toulouse, and Champagne.

When all were assembled, the King was led in, attired in his royal robes, the Sire d'Albert carrying the sword before him, and was conducted to his place in front of the altar. Kneeling, he repeated after the Archbishop the words of the oath usually taken by the kings of France at their coronation, that he would keep and defend the Church, do justice in mercy, maintain peace among his Christian people, suppress all heretics, and expel them from his dominions. This being done, two of the bishops raised the chair in which he was seated, to show him to the people, as if to ask their consent, while two others held the canopy over his head. Then came a blare of trumpets, and an immense shout of "Noel! Noel!"—then the usual acclamation in France at the appearance of the King. The Archbishop proceeded with the service, and anointed him with the *sainte ampoule* (a "holy vessel") of oil, which, according to an old superstition, had been brought from heaven by a dove for the coronation of King Clovis. This part of the ceremony was supposed to render the person of the sovereign sacred and inviolable. The usual prayers, exhortations, and benedictions were pronounced; and as the trumpets again sounded, and the people again shouted "Noel! Noel!" the crown was placed upon the head of Charles the Seventh.

DIFFICULTIES.

Thus had really come to pass the visions which, a few short months before, had flattered the imagination of the Maid of Domremy, and excited the ridicule of warriors and priests, because they knew not the wonderful power of enthusiasm and faith. And thus did she fulfil her twofold promise to the King—the deliverance of Orleans, the capture of Rheims—within three months from the day when she first appeared in arms at Blois.

The holy rites being ended, the Maid threw herself on her knees before the newly-crowned monarch, her eyes streaming with tears of joy and gratitude.

"Gentle King," she said, "now is fulfilled the pleasure of God, whose will it was that I should conduct you to Rheims to be anointed, showing that you are the true King, and he to whom the kingdom of France should belong."

She now regarded her mission as accomplished; she felt that she could no longer trust to any celestial counsel.

"I pray you, gentle King, that you would allow me to return home to my father and mother, keep my flocks and herds as before, and do all things as I was wont to do."

She was insensible to the voice of ambition; indifferent to, or contemptucus of, the pleasures of a court. She had fulfilled her duty nobly, loyally, flinching from neither hardship nor danger; and now she longed for rest.

> "And with many tears implored !
> 'Tis the sound of home restored !
> And as mounts the angel-show,
> Gliding with them she would go,
> But again to stoop below,
> And, returned to grim Lorraine,
> Be a shepherd child again !"

The Maid's request for leave to forsake the wars and retreat to her village home was by no means favourably received. The King and his captains, even whilst themselves distrusting her heavenly mission or supernatural powers, had seen, as Earl Stanhope remarks, how the belief in them had wrought upon the soldiery and the people. They foresaw that in losing her they should lose their best ally. They spared no exertions, no entreaties, to make her forego her thoughts of home, and continue with the army. In this, unhappily, they prevailed. We say "unhappily," for really Jeanne had done her work, had done what she was best fitted to do; she had no military capacity, and all her strength lay in her faith in her mission.

From this time forward, as Sismondi says, it has been observed that Joan still displayed the same courage in enduring pain; that she appeared to feel the same confidence in the good cause of France; but that she no longer seemed to feel the same persuasion that she was acting at the command and under the direct inspiration of Heaven.

The good example set by Troyes and Rheims was quickly followed by Laon, Soissons, Compiègne, Beauvais, and other places of importance. Thus the French drew nearer and yet nearer to the walls of Paris, while the English, although they had recently received some reinforcements from home, were not able to keep the field against them. During this march, however, an evil omen occurred: the Maid's valued sword broke asunder; under what circumstances we shall leave the historian Barante to tell:—

"Victory had made the French arrogant

and thoughtless, so that they resigned themselves to every kind of licentiousness, and nothing could restrain them. They would not listen to the Maid when she reproved them. Her wrath was so far kindled that one day as she met some men-at-arms, who were making merry with a bad woman, she began to smite them with the flat of her sword so hard, that the weapon broke. This was the sword found in the church of Fierbois, and which had just achieved such noble deeds. The loss of it was a grief to everybody, and even to the King. He said to Jeanne, 'You should have taken a good stout stick, and have struck the men with it, instead of risking this sword, which, as you say, came to you by help from Heaven.'"

The King and his army continued their advance towards Paris; and at length, from the heights of St. Denis, the spires and towers of that ancient capital, which for so many centuries has played a prominent part in European history, rose upon their sight. The moment of his coming seemed auspicious, the Duke of Bedford having been summoned away to quiet some dis-

DIFFICULTIES.

turbance in Normandy. An assault was given accordingly in the month of September 1429, and on the same ground now occupied by Rue Travasière. The Maid had urged on the attack, and had predicted, or promised, that on the ensuing night the soldiers should sleep within the city walls. But the King's military fervour had already waned, and he would not be prevailed upon to approach the scene of action nearer than St. Denis. Some of his officers were disspirited by his absence; others were merely jealous of the glory Jeanne had acquired. So it came to pass that her efforts were but badly supported. However, she carried her troops across the first ditch of the city; but the second was broad, deep, and full of water. While sounding it at various parts with her lance, to discover where it might be shallowest, she was sorely wounded by an arrow from the walls. Her standard-bearer was killed by her side. Even then, however, her indomitable spirit would not give the signal for retreat; and from the ground, where she lay prone and helpless, on the side of the first fosse, she continued to stimulate her soldiers, resisting all entreaties to retire until the evening, and then only when the Duke of Orleans had convinced her that the attack had irretrievably failed.

This discomfiture had a great effect upon the mind of the Maid. She regarded it in the light of a warning from Heaven, and dedicating her armour to God before the tents of St. Denis, she resolved upon withdrawing from the wars. But the captains of the royal army, aware of the influence she exercised upon the hearts of the soldiery, besought her most earnestly not to desert her sovereign's cause; and at length she consented. Charles himself made the repulse before Paris an excuse for a retreat to Chinon, to abandon himself to the idle pleasures that, at this time, had so great an attraction for him.

It was an unwise step, and, as Sismondi remarks, everywhere depressed and deadened the enthusiasm of his people. "The unwarlike citizens who, throughout the towns of Champagne, Picardy, and the Isle of France, were now rising or conspiring to

DIFFICULTIES.

throw off the English yoke, well knew that if they failed no mercy would be shown to them, and that they would perish by the hangman's hands; yet they boldly exposed themselves in order to replace their King on his throne; and this King, far from imitating their generosity, could not even bring himself to bear the hardships of a camp or the toils of business for more than two months and a half; he would not any longer consent to forego his festivals, his dances, or his other less innocent delights."

Joan spent the winter chiefly at the royal Court in Bourges, or at Meun-sur-Tarn, in the neighbourhood of Bourges. In December the King granted letters-patent of nobility to her family and herself, with the privilege of bearing the Lily of France for their arms.

When spring returned, hostilities were resumed; and after various successes, the Maid and her captains resolved on attempting the relief of Compiègne, which was then besieged by the Duke of Burgundy. The Maid was suffering greatly from depression, from fear of treachery, and from an inward presentiment that she would fall into the hands of her enemies before the "Feast of St. John." But she did not flinch from her work. With four or five hundred companions, she made her way into Compiègne, without their knowledge of her entrance; and the same evening, reinforced by the garrison, she determined on suddenly assaulting the Burgundian forces (May 24th). She carried her standard, was superbly mounted and equipped, and over her armour wore a mantle of cloth-of-gold.

At the hour appointed for the sally, some of the Burgundian leaders were closely surveying the environs of the city, with the view of detecting some weak point in the ramparts for an assault. From a distance they recognised the noble figure of the Maid, sweeping down upon their camp, with a following of about six hundred men. Immediately they gave the alarm, and brought up a powerful array of Burgundians, who, as the battle went on, were speedily joined by English auxiliaries.

The issue of the fight becoming obvious, a soldier rushed to the Maid, exclaiming,

"Hasten to regain the city, or you and we are all lost!"

"Hold your peace!" cried Jeanne; "think of nothing but of falling on your foes; it depends only on ourselves to discomfit them."

At length, she found herself compelled to give the signal for retreat, herself maintaining the post of honour, and following last in the rear-guard. Never, it is said, had she shown greater valour; but, on approaching the town-gate, she found it partly closed, so that few could pass in together; her soldiers grew confused and dismayed; were more solicitous about their own safety than that of their leader; and her enemies closed round her in a circle. At first she made those before her recoil; and she might, had she been loyally supported, have effected her retreat, but an archer from Picardy, coming up from behind, seized her by her crimson velvet mantle, and drew her from her horse to the ground. She made a fierce effort to rescue herself, but she was overpowered by numbers, and compelled to surrender to Lewis, Count of

Vendôme. Her standard-bearer and her brother Pierre surrendered at the same time, with those of her guard who still survived.

The archer who had captured so rare a prize bade her give him her faith.

"I have sworn [not to escape], and given my faith to another than you, and I shall keep my oath," said Jeanne, and she was led away to the quarters of Jean of Luxembourg.[1]

A few minutes later, the Duke of Burgundy arrived on the scene of battle, and heard the glad tidings. From all sides assembled the English and their allies, filling the air with their cries of triumph. To have captured the Maid was more than to have captured five hundred of the best fighting men in France; for, says Monstrelet, there was neither knight nor captain of war in all King Charles's army whom, up to that day, they had feared so much as they had feared the Maid.

Such was the Duke's sense of the importance of the capture, that he addressed the following letter concerning it to his subjects :—

"By the pleasure of our blessed Creator, the thing has so happened, and such favour has been done us, that she who is called the Maid has been taken, and with her many captains, knights, and squires. Of this capture we are sure there will be everywhere great news, and the error and foolish belief of those who were favourably inclined unto her, will be made known. We write you these tidings, hoping you will have great joy, comfort, and consolation in them, and that you will give thanks and praise to our Creator, who sees and knows all, and who, by His blessed pleasure, deigns to guide most of our enterprises to the good of our lord the King, and the relief of his loyal and good subjects."

CHAPTER V.

THE END.

  . . . . " For me, I know
That I have faithfully obey'd my call,
Confiding not in mine own strength, but His
Who sent me forth to suffer and to do
His will; and in that faith I shall appear
Before the just tribunal of that God
Whom grateful love has taught me to adore !"
    SOUTHEY, *Joan of Arc*, B. ix.

"A thorough and earnest persuasion that hers was the rightful cause—that in all she had said she spoke the truth—that in all she did she was doing her duty—a courage that did not shrink before embattled armies, or beleaguered walls, or judges thirsting for her blood—a most resolute will on all points that were connected with her mission—perfect meekness and humility on all that were not—a clear, plain sense, that would confound the casuistry of sophists—a dutiful devotion on all points to her country and her God. Such was the character of Jeanne d'Arc."—EARL STANHOPE, *Joan of Arc*.

THE captive heroine was transferred successively to the prisons of Beaurevoir, Arras, and Le Crotry. Twice she attempted to break from her bonds. On the first occasion she had succeeded in forcing a passage through the wall, but was arrested on her way, and afterwards imprisoned in a still more secluded dungeon. The second time she flung herself headlong from the summit of her prison tower, but was taken up senseless on the ground. She declared at her trial that her "Voices" had dissuaded her from this attempt, but had brought consolation to her under its failure.

The English, however, showed a great eagerness to get the prisoner into their own hands; and, in the month of November 1430, purchased her from John of Luxembourg for a sum of ten thousand livres. The cruel treatment she received at the hands of the English is well described by Barante:—

" Jeanne was now removed to Rouen, where there resided the young King, Henry VI., and all the English leaders. She was led into the great tower of the castle; an iron cage was made for her, and her feet were secured by a chain. The English archers who guarded her treated her with gross contumely, and more than once with the most shameful violence. Nor was it only the common soldiers who thus behaved. The Sire de Luxembourg, whose prisoner she had been, happening to pass through Rouen, went to see her in her prison, accompanied by the Earls of Warwick and Stafford. 'Jeanne,' said one of them in jest, 'I am come to put you to ransom, but you will have to promise never again to bear arms against us.' 'Oh! *mon Dieu*, you were laughing at me,' said she; 'you have neither the will nor the power to ransom me. I know well that the English will cause me to die, thinking that after my death they will win back the kingdom of France. But even were they a hundred thousand Goddams[1] more than they are they shall never have this kingdom.' Incensed at these words, the Earl of Stafford drew his dagger to strike her, but was prevented by the Earl of Warwick."

Jeanne was doomed to death, and she knew it. Nor, if she had been put to death as a prisoner of war, who had tried to escape, should we have had any ground to accuse

[1] This was the nickname given to our English soldiers, in allusion to their bad habit of swearing.

her captors, judging them from the point of view of the age in which they lived. The French had been guilty of atrocities worse than this. But the real disgrace of the Maid's enemies is, that they not only sought to pour out their vengeance upon her for their successive defeats, but that they endeavoured to discredit and blacken her in the opinion of her contemporaries, and the eyes of posterity. They tried to brand her as " a disciple and limb of the fiend which used false enchantments and sorcery," and to damage the cause of Charles VII., by linking it with a witch's name. With a degree of injustice which even now-a-days makes an Englishman bend his head in shame, they abandoned their claim upon her as a prisoner of war, to assert that she was their subject; and they brought her before an ecclesiastical judgment-seat on the charge of witchcraft. On this tribunal, however, it is some consolation to reflect that no Englishman sat. The first judge was a Frenchman, the Bishop of Beauvais; and the second, Jean Lemaitre, Vicar-General of the Inquisition, was also a Frenchman; and the office of prosecutor devolved upon another Frenchman, Estivet, a canon of Beauvais. The tribunal thus formed held its sittings at Rouen, and was assisted by the advice of nearly one hundred doctors of theology.

"Unjustifiable," says Earl Stanhope, "as this trial appears in its general scope and design, it was further darkened in its progress by many acts of fraud and violence, and an evident predetermination to condemn. A private investigation, similar to those at Poitiers, and with the same result, having been appointed, the Duke of Bedford is said to have concealed himself in a neighbouring apartment, and looked on through a rent in the wall. A priest, named Nicolas l'Oiseleur, was instructed to enter Joan's prison, to represent himself as her countryman from Lorraine, and as a sufferer in the cause of King Charles; thus, it was hoped, gaining upon her confidence, giving her false counsels, and betraying her, under the seal of confession, into some unguarded disclosures. A burgher of Rouen was sent to Domremy to gather some accounts of her early life; but, as these proved uniformly favourable, they were suppressed at the trial. In like manner, many answers tending to her vindication were garbled or omitted in the written reports. She was allowed neither counsel nor advisers. In short, every artifice was used to entrap, every threat to overawe, an untaught and helpless girl."

Jeanne was brought before her judges for the first time on the 21st of February 1431. The scene was the castle chapel at Rouen, and she appeared in her usual military garb, but loaded with chains. She was subjected to no less than fifteen examinations; but she failed not from first to last; was always clear, prompt, and resolute; neither yielded to menaces nor promises; and never once was entrapped into an admission which falsified the tenor of her whole life. But not only did she display a wonderful resolution and promptitude; she showed, too, an extraordinarily clear and sagacious intellect, which completely baffled the subtlety of her inquisitorial tyrants. Thus, she was asked whether she believed herself to be in the grace of God? Had she answered "Yes," she would have been accused of ignorance and presumption; had she answered "No," she would have been declared guilty by her own confession. "It is a difficult matter to reply to such a question," said Jeanne. "So difficult," interposed one of the hundred assessors, moved to compassion, "that the prisoner is not bound in law to answer it." "You had better be silent," shouted the Bishop, and, turning to Jeanne, he repeated the question. "If I am not in the grace of God," she answered, "I pray God that it may be vouchsafed to me; if I am, I pray God that I may be preserved in it."

It will be impossible for us, and not to the edification of our readers, that we should follow up, day after day, the prosecution of the unhappy Maid. And yet some of the incidents of the trial were so full of interest, and many of them illuminate so clearly the beautiful character of the victim, that we cannot pass them over. The reader must recollect that the great object of her judges was to prove her guilty of witchcraft; and this they attempted to do by connecting her with a certain "Fairies' Tree" in Domremy, and with the banner which she bore in battle. As to the first, her answer was, that she had often been round the tree in procession with other village maidens, but had never beheld any of her visitations at that spot. In reference to the banner, she explained, that she carried it in battle in preference to spear or sword; that she wished not to kill any one with her own hand, and that she never had.

Q. "When you first took this banner, did you ask whether it would make you victorious in every battle?"

A. "The Voices told me to take it without fear, and that God would assist me."

Q. "Which gave the greater help—you to the banner, or the banner to you?"

A. "Whether victory came from the banner or from me, it belonged to our Lord alone."

Q. "Was the hope of victory founded on the banner or yourself?"

A. "It was founded on God, and on nought besides."

Q. "If another person had borne it, would the same success have ensued?"

A. "I cannot tell: I refer myself to God."

Q. "Why were you chosen sooner than another?"

A. "It was the pleasure of God that thus a simple maid should put the foes of the King to flight."

Q. "Were you not wont to say, to encourage the soldiers, that all the standards made in resemblance of your own would be fortunate?"

A. "I used to say to them, 'Rush in boldly among the English,' and then I used to rush in myself."

Here is another passage well worth reading:—

Q. "At what hour did you last eat and drink?"

A. "Since yesterday afternoon, I have not eaten or drunk anything."

Q. "How long is it since you heard the Voice that comes to you?"

A. "I heard it yesterday, and I have heard it again to-day."

Q. "At what hour did you hear it yesterday?"

A. "I heard it three times; once in the morning, once in the evening, and the third time when the *Ave Maria* was singing. I hear it much oftener than I can tell you."

Q. "What were you doing yesterday morning when the *Voice* came to you?"

A. "I was sleeping, and it awoke me."

Q. "Did it wake you by touching your arm?"

A. "No, it woke me without touching me."

Q. "Was the voice in your chamber?"

A. "Not that I know of, but it was in the castle."

Q. "Did you kneel then, and thank the Voice?"

A. "I thanked it, sitting up in my bed, and clasping my hands."

Q. "Why did it come?"

A. "Because I had asked its help."

Q. "And what did it bid you do?"

A. "It bade me answer you boldly."

Q. "What did it say to you at the moment it woke you?"

A. "I begged its counsel on what I ought to answer, praying it to inquire of God. And the Voice told me to answer you boldly, and God would help me."

Jeanne then broke out into an indignant

remonstrance with the Bishop, whom she half declared was her enemy and not her judge. "Be mindful what you do," said she, "for really I am sent on the part of God, and you are getting yourself in great danger."

"The King has commanded me to make your trial, and I shall make it."

At the first sitting, the examination was as follows:—

Q. "Will you in your visions see St. Michael and the angels corporeally and really?"

A. "I saw them with my bodily eyes as well as I see you. When they left me I wept, and fain would I that they had borne me away with them."

Q. "What did St. Michael say to you the first time he appeared?"

A. "I have not permission yet to tell you. . . . I may by and bye. I told my King what had been revealed to me, because it regarded him. I wish you had a copy of that book at Poitiers."

Q. "Did God command you to dress as a man?"

A. "My man's dress is a very trifling

matter, the most trifling. I did not put it on by the advice of any man in the world. Whatever I have done of good, I have done by command of God and the saints. ... I would rather have been torn by wild horses than have come into France without the permission of God. ... If He ordered me to put on another habit, I should put it on. ... In all that I have done according to His will, I believe that I have done well, and, therefore, I look for His good keeping and good help."

Her interrogators next proceeded to inquire why her great hopes for her country had not been fulfilled, if she really were, as she pretended, guided by divine inspiration:—

A. "Before seven years are at end, the English shall abandon a greater gage than they abandoned before Orleans, and they shall lose all in France. ... Greater ruin shall come upon them than ever they have had yet, and it shall be by a victory that God will give the French."

Q. "How do you know this?"

A. "I know it by the revelation that has

been made to me. Before seven years are over, it shall come to pass; and very wroth am I that it is so long delayed."

Q. "On what day will it happen?"

A. "I know neither the day nor the hour."

Q. "In what year?"

A. "That I shall not tell you. Would it might happen before Midsummer!"

Q. "Did you not say to John Grey, your guard, that it would happen before Martinmas?"

A. "I said to him that many things would be seen before Martinmas, and that perhaps it would be the English who should be cast down to the English ground."

Q. "Who has informed you that this event is to take place?"

A. "St. Catharine and St. Margaret."

A great many questions were now put to her respecting the appearance of these saints. She said:—

"I see them always in the same form. . . . I see a face. . . . I cannot tell you whether anything in the shape of arms or body is visible. . . . They are crowned, but of their vestments I cannot speak. . . . I know them by the sound of their sweet and holy voices. . . . They speak clearly, and in beautiful language, and I understand them perfectly."

Q. "Does St. Margaret speak English?"

A. "How should she speak English when she is not of the English party?"

Q. "With respect to the crowned heads which you see, have they rings in their ears?"

A. "I do not know."

Q. "Have you not yourself some rings?"

A. [To the Bishop.] "You have one that is mine, and the Burgundians have another."

Q. "Who gave you the ring which the Burgundians have?"

A. "My father and mother at Domremy. The words *Jhesus Maria* are written on it. My brother gave me the other ring that *you* have, and I charge you to deliver it to the Church."

Q. "Did St. Katherine and St. Margaret ever converse with you under the fairy tree?"

A. "I know not."

Q. "Did they ever speak to you by the fountain over that tree?"

A. "Yes. I have heard them in that place, but I do not know what they then said to me." (And why? Because her enthusiastic mind had not yet given reality to its early visions.)

Q. "What have those saints promised you, there or elsewhere?"

A. "That concerns not the present trial. ... But, amongst other things, they tell me that my King shall assuredly recover his kingdom; and me they have promised to guide to Paradise, as I have prayed of them. They promise me nothing but by the permission of God."

Q. "Has your *counsel* (the Voices) promised that you shall be delivered out of prison?"

A. "Ask me three months hence, and I will answer you."

Q. "Have your *Voices* forbidden you to speak the truth?"

A. "Would you have me tell what is made known only to the King of France?

I know many things that do not concern this trial. . . . I know that the King shall recover all his territories in France; this do I know as certainly as that you are here. Oh, I should die but for the revelation that consoles me every day!"

Who but must sympathize with this hapless victim, whose only crime was her patriotism, whose only delusion one that sprung from high motives, acting on an excited fancy,—who but must sympathize with her, as, day after day, she was thus subjected to the cruel questioning of doctors and bishops,—she, the gentle, the womanly, the undefended,—standing before judges who had already made up their minds to condemn her, and in a court crowded with enemies?

Our space will permit us to give but one more specimen of the meaningless persecution to which she was exposed, and of the calmness and composure with which she endured it.

Q. "Did you *inquire* of your Voices whether, by virtue of your standard, you would win all the battles you fought?"

A. "The Voices told me to take the standard in the name of God, to carry it bravely, and God would help me!"

Q. "Was your hope of victory founded on your standard or yourself?"

A. "It was founded on God, and on none other."

Q. "Do you think that if you were married, your *Voices* would still come to you?"

A. "I know not; I leave all to God."

Q. "Do you believe your King did well to kill, or cause to be killed, the Lord Duke of Burgundy?"

A. "It was a great loss to his kingdom; but whatever occurred between them, God sent *me* to the help of the King of France."

Q. "Why did you like to look at your ring on which *Jhesus Maria* was written, when you set out on any expedition?"

A. "For love and honour of my father and mother, who gave it me; and because, having it on my hand, I trusted St. Catherine, who appears to me."

Q. "When you hung garlands on the tree

of your village, were they offerings to those who appear to you?"

A. "No."

Q. "When your saints come, do you revere them by kneeling and bowing?"

A. "Yes, I adore them with all due honour; for I know that they belong to the kingdom of Paradise."

It is needless to say that this protracted trial proved nothing. But her judges had bound and pledged themselves to her condemnation, and they laid before the University of Paris, which in all haste confirmed them, twelve charges of heresy and witchcraft. On the 24th of May 1431, exactly a twelvemonth after her capture, she was exposed to the public gaze upon a platform, and under threat of instant death, compelled to sign a recantation of her error. Her courage failed her for awhile, and she signed! Sentence was then passed upon her, namely, that out of grace and moderation her life should be spared, but that the remainder of it would be spent in prison, "with the bread of grief and the water of anguish for her food."

It was Jeanne's hope that she would now be handed over to the French, under whose charge she knew and felt she would be safe from further molestation. But her enemies carried her back to the prison she had already occupied, determined to find or invent some pretext for further progress. She had promised to resume a female dress; but, we are told that, one night, a suit of man's apparel was placed in her cell, and her own dress removed, so that in the morning she was forced to clothe herself in the forbidden garments. Another account relates that she did so to protect herself from insult and injury of the basest kind.

At all events, the end of her enemies was attained. They publicly announced that she had relapsed into heresy and sorcery, and that no pardon would now be granted. In this atrocious action the Bishop of Beauvais was the principal actor.

At daybreak, on the 30th of May, her confessor, Martin l'Advenu entered her cell, with the sad tidings that she was to be burned alive that very day in the marketplace of Rouen. Who will wonder that at first her firmness gave way? that she shed tears of agony, and tore her hair, imploring God to help her against her enemies? But she now recovered her usual calm and dignified demeanour, and having made her last confession to the priest, received the Holy Sacrament from his hands.

She was then attired in the gloomy garb prescribed for relapsed heretics; and on her head was set a kind of mitre, inscribed in large letters with the words—" HÉRÉTIQUE, RELAPSE, APOSTATE, IDOLATRE!"

Her confessor and another priest mounted the car which was to bear her to the place of execution. As it was on the point of moving, the monk L'Oiseleur, who had acted as a spy upon her, and a witness against her, heart-stricken with remorse, forced his way through the escort of English soldiers, and climbing up, flung himself at the feet of the Maid, imploring her pardon. Before she could grant it, the soldiers dragged him away, and the Earl of Warwick advised him, if he valued his life, to make haste out of Rouen.

It is said that ten thousand persons were

present at her martyrdom, but afraid to manifest their pity from fear of their English masters. The ecclesiastical judges and civil magistrates were in their places, together with Cardinal Beaufort, of England, the Bishop of Thourenne and Noyon, and most of the doctors and lawyers who had assisted at her trial.

After Jeanne had arrived at the place of execution, and been conducted to the scaffold, she was doomed to listen to a long sermon from one of her persecutors, and then her sentence was publicly read.

Jeanne now fell on her knees, weeping, to offer up her last prayers to God. And these were uttered so earnestly and tenderly, and breathed so generous and charitable a spirit, that the multitude, and many even of her judges, were moved to tears.

She asked for a cross, and at the request of an attendant priest, a crucifix was sent for from St. Saviour's Church. Meantime, an English soldier, more compassionate than his fellows, broke his staff asunder, and hastily fashioned with the fragments a rude cross, which the Maid clasped joyfully to her breast.

But the other soldiers began to murmur at the long delay. "Come, you priests," they exclaimed, "do you mean to make us dine here?" They grew so impatient that two officials ascended the scaffold, and a voice cried hastily, "Take her away! take her away!" She was then borne by the press of the soldiery to the pile. Several of the priests and assessors then fled from the scene, protesting against the severity with which the judgment they had pronounced against her was to be carried out. The executioner himself shrank from his cruel task, partly on account of her great renown, and partly from the cruel way in which he had been ordered to bind her *above* the fuel, so that when the flames were kindled he would be unable to reach her mercifully to hasten her death.

What ensued, we shall now describe in the words of Miss Harriet Parr:—

The Bishop of Beauvais came down from his tribunal, and confronted her, apparently expecting she would denounce the King, who had made no effort to deliver her, or make some appeal for mercy. But she only said:

"Bishop, I die by you! Had you placed me in the hands of the Church, I had never come here!"

The two monks who attended her, kneeling, weeping, and praying, did not perceive the fire creeping up. But *she* did, and she bade them go down. "And hold aloft the crucifix before me, and speak loud enough for me to hear you, until I die," she exclaimed; and thus was left, calling upon Christ and His saints, and looking up to the blue unconscious heavens above her.

"When the fire touched her, she shuddered, and cried, '*Water! holy water!*' then '*Jesus! Jesus!*' For a little while all the air from earth to heaven throbbed with the prayer of her anguish—'*Jesus! Jesus!*' The eyes of the people were dazzled and dim. Some saw the name of the Redeemer written in the eddying furnace-blast; others saw a white dove hovering in the smoke of her sacrifice.

"Brother Martin (one of her attendants), standing almost in the draft of the flames, heard her sob with a last sublime effort of faith, bearing her witness to God whom she

trusted: '*My Voices have not deceived me!*'
And then came death, and with great victory delivered her. 'JESUS!' with a very loud voice she cried again; and her spirit passed.

"For a moment there was silence. Then —'Draw back the fire, and show her *dead* to the people, that none may ever say she has escaped!'

'The soldiers stared aghast; hoarse mutterings of indignation rolled through the crowd.

"' She was unjustly condemned—unjustly condemned!'
"' *She now is in the hand of God.*'"

Thus perished, in her twentieth year, the tender, true, and loyal Jeanne d'Arc, known through all times as the Maid of Orleans, and as one of the brightest, bravest, and noblest heroines whom history has ever celebrated. Let us learn the lesson of her life: and that is, unflinchingly, courageously, and prayerfully, to do the work which God imposes upon each one of us. Our mission may not be so sublime as that which God intrusted to the Maid; but each of us *has* a mission.

and, rightly understood, a mission which must hereafter prove of benefit to our fellows.

We conclude this sketch of her remarkable career with the character drawn of her by a well-qualified judge, Thomas Carlyle:—

Considered, says Carlyle, as an object of poetry or history, Jeanne d'Arc, the most singular personage of modern times, presents a character capable of being viewed under a great variety of aspects, and with a corresponding variety of emotions. To the English of her own age, bigoted in their creed, and baffled by her prowess, she appeared inspired by the devil, and was naturally burnt as a sorceress. In this light, too, she is painted in the poems of Shakespeare. To Voltaire, again, whose trade it was to war with any kind of superstition, this child of fanatic ardour served no better than a moonstruck zealot; and the people who followed her, and believed in her, something worse than lunatics. The glory of what she had achieved was forgotten, when the means of achieving it were recollected; and the Maid of Orleans was deemed the fit subject of a poem, the wittiest and most profligate for which literature has to blush.

Such a manner, continues Carlyle, of considering the Maid of Orleans is evidently not the right one. Feelings so deep and earnest as hers can never be an object of ridicule; whoever pursues a purpose of any art with such genial devotedness, is entitled to awaken emotions, at least of a serious kind, in the hearts of others. Enthusiasm puts on different shapes in every different age: always in some degree outlived, often it is dangerous; its very essence is a tendency to error and exaggeration, yet it is the fundamental quality of strong souls; the true nobility of blood, in which all greatness of thought or action has its use. *Quicquid vult valdè vult*[1] is even the first and surest test of mental capability. This peasant girl, who felt within her such fiery vehemence of resolution, that she could subdue the minds of kings and captains to her will, and lead armies on to battle, conquering, till her country was cleared of its invaders, must

[1] That is, whatever one wills, one should will firmly.

evidently have possessed the elements of a majestic character. Benevolent feeling, sublime ideas, and, above all, an overpowering will, are here undoubtedly marked. Nor does the form, which her activity assumed, seem less adapted for displaying these qualities, than many other forms in which we praise them. Jeanne d'Arc must have been a creature of shadowy yet far-glancing dreams of unutterable feelings, of "thoughts that wandered through eternity." Who can tell the trials and the triumphs, the splendours and the terrors, of which her simple spirit was the scene?

Hers were errors, but errors which a generous soul alone could have committed, and which generous souls would have done more than pardon. Her darkness and delusions were of the understanding only; they but make the radiance of her heart more touching and apparent; as clouds are gilded by the sun's light into something more beautiful than the azure itself.

It is in this light, young readers, you should learn to consider the character of Jeanne the Maid. Put aside her mental delusions—those visions and voices which were created by an intense imagination continually brooding upon one great theme—and she stands before you as one of the brightest women whose names adorn the page of history. So pure, so gentle; so patient under adversity, so moderate in prosperity; passing through the roughest scenes, and among the warriors and courtiers of a corrupted age, as the Three Children passed through the fire unburned; sensible of all sweet domestic feelings; generous, and trustful, and loyal, she seems, as we gaze upon her,

> "A creature all too fair and good
> For human nature's daily food."[1]

We may learn, as we have said, a lesson from her career; namely, to set duty before us as the paramount aim of our lives; to do what seems to be our duty with all our heart, and soul, and strength, in humble, prayerful trust in God; and so, perchance, it may come to be written upon our tombs as the true expression of all our aspira-

[1] Wordsworth.

tions, struggles and success, that the life of each one of us—whatever our condition—proved to be, " a Noble Purpose Nobly Won."[1]

[1] The title of a very beautiful romance, founded on the life of Jeanne d'Arc, by Miss Manning.

www.ingramcontent.com/pod-product-compliance
Lightning Source LLC
Chambersburg PA
CBHW020144170426
43199CB00010B/881